Poems for all

Joseph parambil

BookLeaf Publishing

Presentation by *BookLeaf Publishing*

Web: www.bookleafpub.com

E-mail: info@bookleafpub.com

ISBN: 9789357211246

First edition 2022

DEDICATION

For

my parents and siblings

ACKNOWLEDGEMENT

I acknowledge the support and care provided by my parents, sister and friends who have greatly encouraged me to pursue my dreams of writing a book. I also acknowledge the contribution of all my teachers through the years who have taught me what I have learnt so far.

PREFACE

I chose to write this book for people to enjoy.

The moneyman

My name is Dan, the money man.
My dad used to be the local milk man
I am now a big businessman
Now listen to the masterplan

I had to receive education
Never did I make a miscalculation
In my thoughts rang the words more precision
And through all this I saw the revelation

It was all because of the federation
The homeless the lonely and the inflation
At the end of this road was damnation
To escape this required total dedication

The problem was lack of equity
My town was struck with poverty
My dad thought and bought some property
I got stuck and thought properly

A couple of deals later
I became a solid cash generator
My brain was a mass calculator
My next plan was to become a dictator

I had the cash
I had grown a fine moustache
The reasoning came like a flash
The system was soon to be abashed

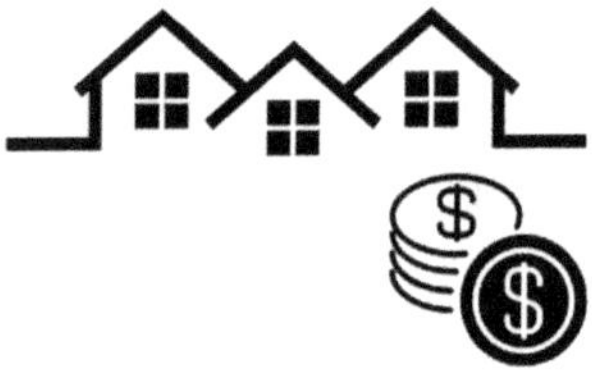

The tombstones

Walking past the tombstone
I think I lost my phone-
I can start to feel
Cold inside my bone

The graveyard seems a bit cold
All you can see is moss
As I keep walking
I visualise a cross

And on this cross I can see
A bloody man staring right at me
I look around in shock and fright
I think I just lost my appetite

I turn around, run and cry
Leave me alone I don't want to die
Nevertheless, they move and turn
This journey is taking a downturn

I'm nearly surrounded
Well, these tombstones seem well-grounded
I could climb on one and then try climb a tree
But I have a feeling the undead might disagree

I leap onto the stone
Eluding hands of bone
But as I try clambering
I lose my footing

I fell back down
The undead were happy
They swarmed me and gained their crown
As I was left unhappy

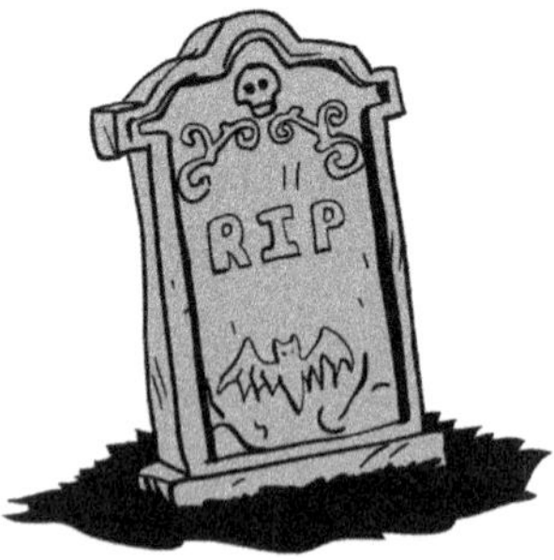

Society

The society we live in is dysfunctional
All the rules, laws; they're destructible
The government is incapable
If you think about it my logic is untouchable

All the common folk are gullible
Even taxes now are deductible
No good man can hide from the law
In my opinion dystopia is the devil's claw

Honestly, I'd rather be an outlaw
But sadly, nobody can withdraw
This world is a massive jigsaw
Its time I hack it with a chainsaw

I'd like to go back to the default
Where people spiced meat with rock salt
But sadly, saying that is EZ
The common folk think like NPC's

The parliament is committing assault
Locking all our money into their vaults

I think it's time to change
My proposition is to revolt

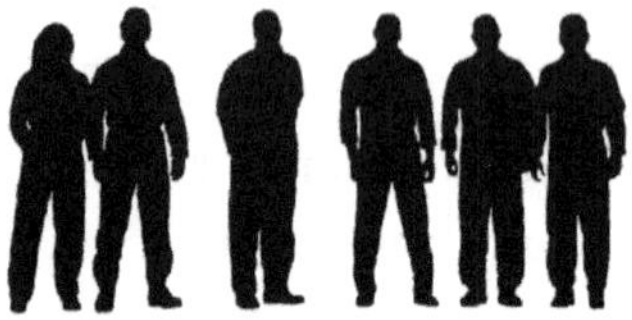

Leviathan

I was with my crew
Doing what we liked to do
Then we passed the Baltic sea
A feeling aroused in me
I was shaken to the core
This was something unlike ever before

Our lookout screamed
Pointing at a few rocks near shore
I looked and it kind of seemed
The bumps were moving towards us all
I took my specs and put them on
All my happiness was now gone
A scary phenomenon
known as the beast of Babylon

I sail on my own
broken, shattered and now all alone
I once had a crew
Swallowed up and now I am all through

I can sense the seas
I know what lays down in the deep

But whilst he lays and dreams
I am on the watch for marines

Me and my ship are the only ones
Left to sing our lonely song
Just me and the broken mast
Plus, all the treasure I had amassed
I sometimes wished for something more
I hate me and my visions of grandeur

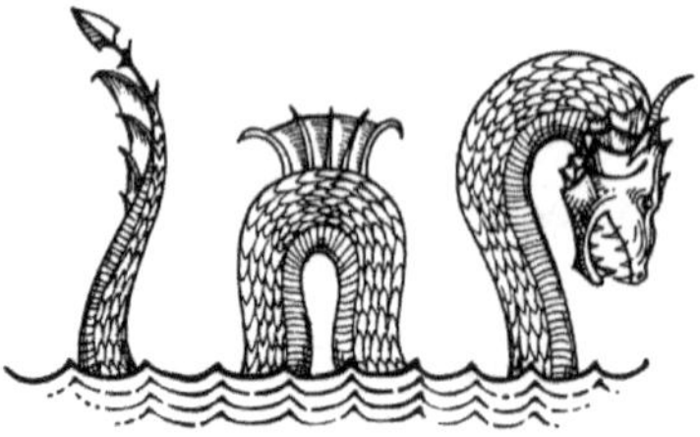

Life and nature

I am walking in the park
I can hear the birds
I spot a little stark
Nature cannot be summarised in words

However, I will do my best
You'll have to interpret the rest
Of mother nature's big plan
For you, a glorified cave man

It all starts at birth
Your body was made from earth
Dust you are and dust you shall return to
You are flawed but we'll just have to make do

Drinking from a king's cup
say bottoms up
It feels like life was a warmup
Thinking's now got you wound up
You were a mistake from the get up

Now that you’ve realised you're mad
You’ve started to go mad
And as you let out your last breath
You're consumed by death.

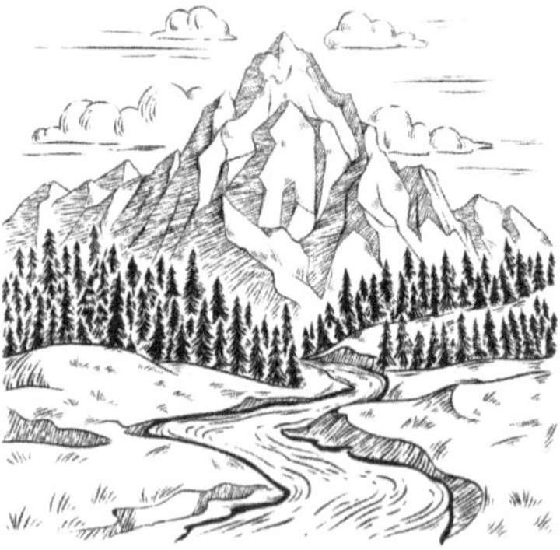

God

God is real
God is fake
God could just be a rake
God has lived
God has died
God is an entity in who we confide

God is inside
God is outside
God is there when we're unsatisfied
God is happy
God is sad
God is there when things go bad

God says hello
God says bye
God is there when things go wry
God says good morning
God says good night
God doesn't care if your black or white

God makes the gaps
God fills the gaps
God will help you when you collapse

God is with you
God is with me
God loves his devotees

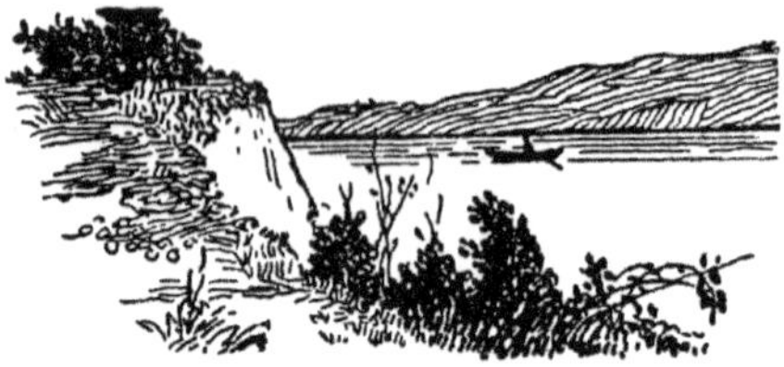

The goddess of wisdom

The first child from a man
This was never Zeus's plan
Had a long attention span
This was never said in the scan

The mother was Metis
To her goes all the credits
The child will be better
And The world would never forget her

She shall be wise
Seeing through man's lies
She was like an oracle
Allegorical, Metaphorical and Historical.

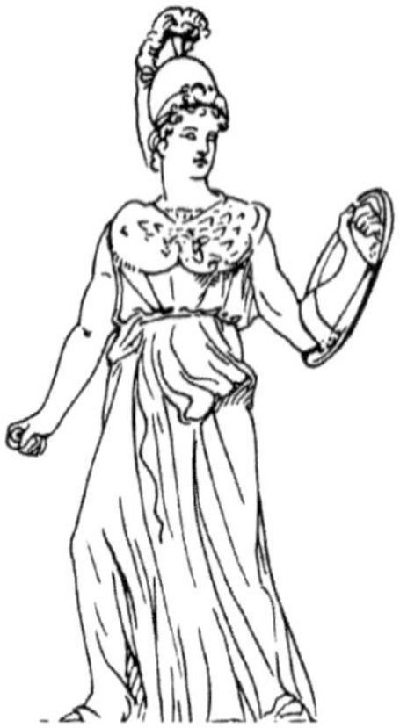

Hippopotomonstrosesquipped aliophobia

This subject is of mass irrelevance
The bars I'm spitting, they might even be
venomous
there is massive circumstantial evidence
you're faulty artificial intelligence

You've all been leaching off my benevolence
So its time to show a little bit of unpleasantness
This ain't no inelegant overemphasis
I'm just displaying my intelligence

What your afraid of is worse than arachnophobia
more complicated than triskaidekaphobia
More odd than the ominous onomatophobia
If your wondering, you have
Hippopotomonstrosesquippedaliophobia

Imagine what it'd be like to be you
the conditions that torment and slowly try break
through
After five seconds I'd honestly be through

hate me hate you, hate life
ain't got nothing to live up to

So don't laugh and try to interfere
for all you know they could be drowning in tears
As they're sat they listening to you leer
about something they could not control
their very worst fear

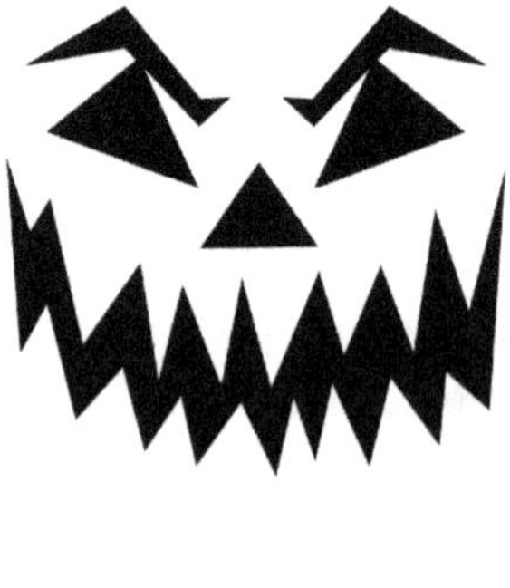

The loop

At the beginning we have the big bang
A massive boom from which all the planets
sprang
Then as everything starts to settle down
Life began up in our home town

Earth-the planet of blue and green
Venus- a beautiful place it had once been
Mars- Water it may see
and lastly we have the fire known as mercury

Now you will see life progress
from cells to a human in a dress
The dinosaurs are now long gone
the meteor that destroyed them feels as far away
as the sun

We are advancing
We have passed ritual dancing
In advancement we've passed a cornerstone
From the wheel, to high heels and now the cell
phone

But then as our civilisation becomes relaxed
There is a fear of a future collapse
The negative magnetic pole
is pointing at an incoming black hole

Suddenly as we're being sucked in
Time rewinds and we are here again
Stuck in a loop is frustrating
and our race still doesn't know anything

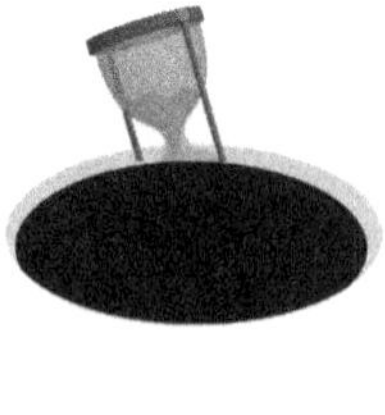

The boss

Oh we failed our job
The house that we were supposed to rob
Is left safe and sound
All we got was a pound
From the ground it came
We can't hide our shame
Oh what will he say
Oh what will he say

We may be screwed
He's got a monstrous attitude
Oh we are fools
We should have stuck to the rules
Now what can we do
I have no clue
Oh god we are through
Oh god we are through

He's gunna pull out some guns
Oh theres gonna be tons

I have an idea
How bout we go rob IKEA
Sneek in and try
But fail and we'll die-
Oh god we better be fast
Better be fast

Welp turns out we got caught
Im starting to get second thoughts
Oh god what shall we do
I wish i had withdrew.

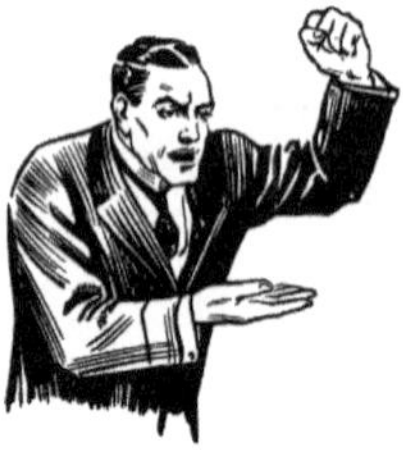

The pomegranate tree

There once was a girl named Persephone
The crops she tended to oversee
Other than that she was carefree

Her mother was Demeter
She was an plant seeder
To mankind she was a feeder

The father was Zeus
he loved grape juice and women he would seduce
When Persephone went missing he looked for an excuse

The betrothed was hades
Usually not known for the ladies
His dog Cerberus ain't got rabies
But is known for the brain of a baby

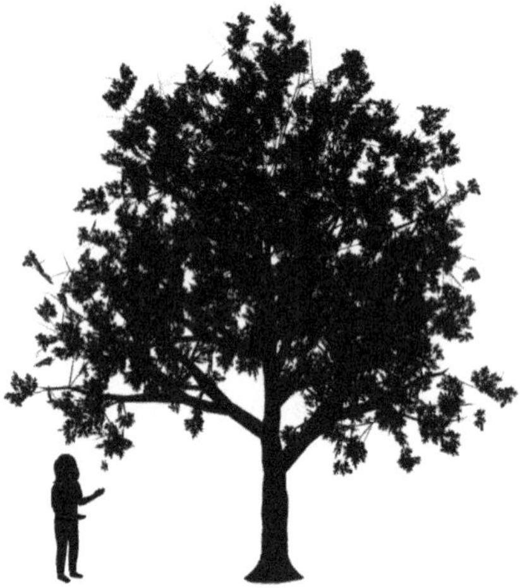

Phones

Pocket PC's
Helps the community
One is enough
None would be tough
Even 7 year olds have them
So go get one

Nature

The sky is blood red
I'm lying on a grass bed
I want to be dead

That was a haiku but this is a Tanka,
and it is not from sri lanka, its from the land of
the Fujiyama called japan.

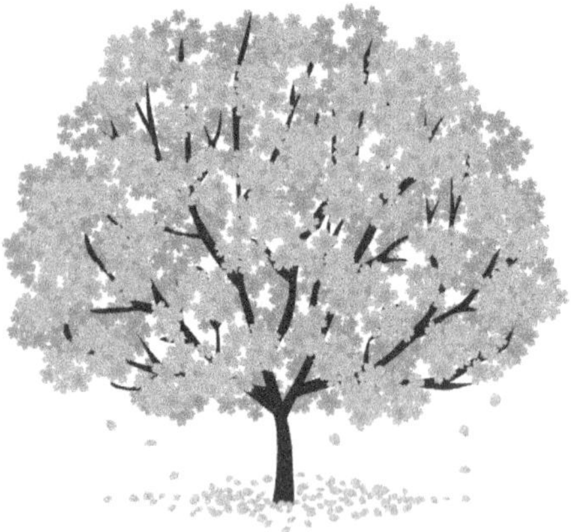

Spots and stripes

Spots and stripes
there are so many types
from pool balls to fashion
I think I may have found my passion

you can have polka dots
or facial spots
decorative pots
or maybe cool rooftops

Now moving onto stripes
time to get rid of the stereotypes
From coloured pipes
to the shoes from Nikes

Some may says its retro
But with these I'm gonna hop on the metro
I really don't know what your on about bro
with these spots and stripes I looped drippy though

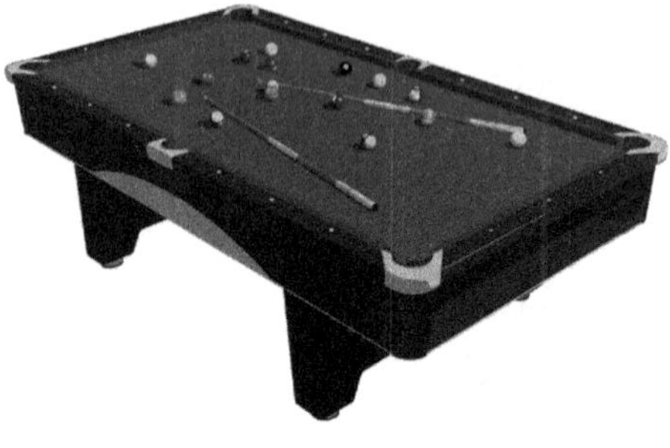

Rust

Rust is what goes on iron
In this little equation there are no ions
It's almost the opposite of abrasion
This is a very important equation

If iron comes in contact with either of these
it will turn into rust with maximum ease
if left long enough
then the reaction will stop sure enough

But by the end of all this
your clean iron you will miss
because it will be covered from head to toe
in the stuff known as rust bro

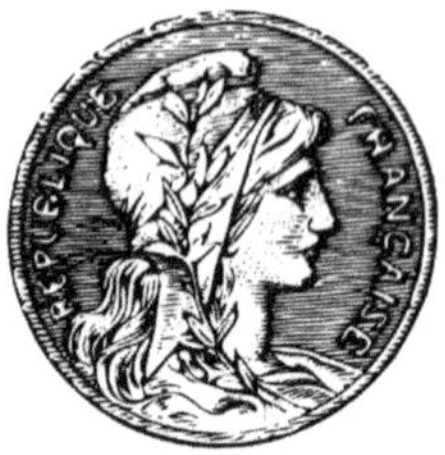

Calculations

I was asked by the international association
to find out the hidden calculation
save them and all their corporations
by using my brain and education

For so long I could have been dominating
Nobody could beat me at high class debating
But even still I've been alternating
between concentrating on skills and mandarin translating

I work as a translator in the daytime
but when it hits night
I focus in the street light
I love night time over daytime
Because I can learn more and some skills i can refine

So when i was asked
to take on this task
i was more than joyed

i couldn't wait to get employed
A quite decent pay is more than I could ask
So I accepted and took a sip from my flask

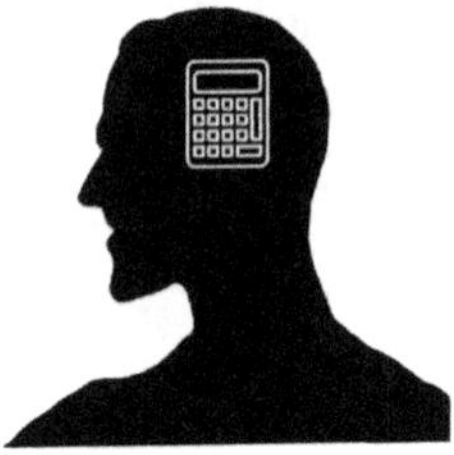

The ideal poem

The ideal poem would have to be
made by one who must see
rhyming words are not good alone
they have to have meaning from blood and bone

You have to know what your writing for
A relative, friend or because of what you swore
To make a poem is hard you see
you must think what will its topic be

Now after thinking of meaning
Some words might need some screening
Look through your poem and start some
cleaning
Take it all in, absorb the feeling

Now what you've gotta do
Sweep through your poem, it should rhyme
through and through
And because you've got your meaning down
You can sit back and relax, head with a crown

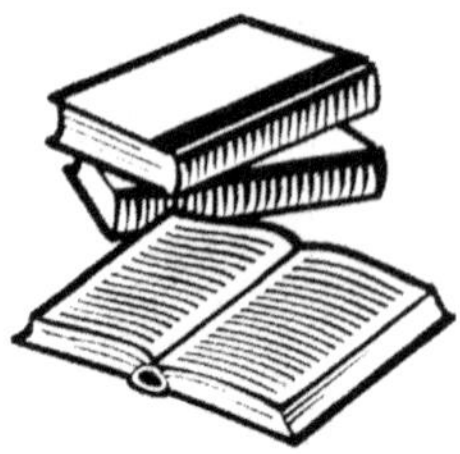

Weather ain't lookin' too good

I think there should be a ban
On the opportunities offered to man
if any other animal had this
they would acquire bliss

So what do we do now
we can't stop, we cant back down
The methane coming from a cow
is enough to pollute a room with a clown

Now what could we ever do
you cant stop a cow from taking a poo
Converters, thats all we need
Take action quickly before our planet bleeds!

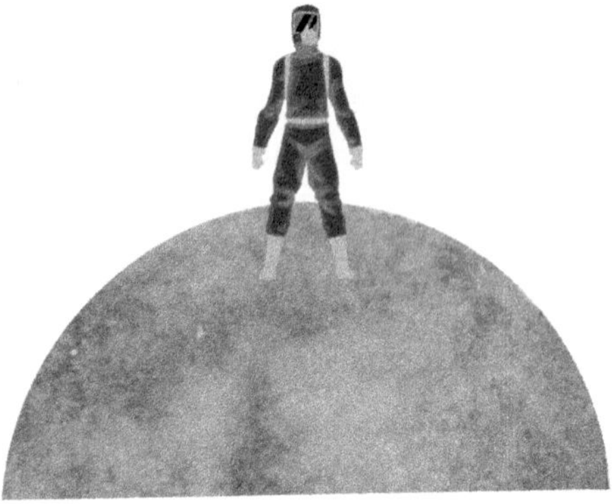

Siblings

Oh the pain of a sibling
Something you wouldn't understand
Sisters, brothers, younger or older
Never a helping hand

Now what do you do when they come to you
asking for assistance
After all the torture they've put you through
Ask them for some consistence?

The answer would be you help them out, only
just a bit
Slowly amass until they rely on you and then
you simply quit
They need to learn on their own, you would be
helping them out
but at the time, they'd scream and cry, roll
around and shout

But keep in mind your helping them, through the
good and bad

So when they beg for your help, do not get really mad

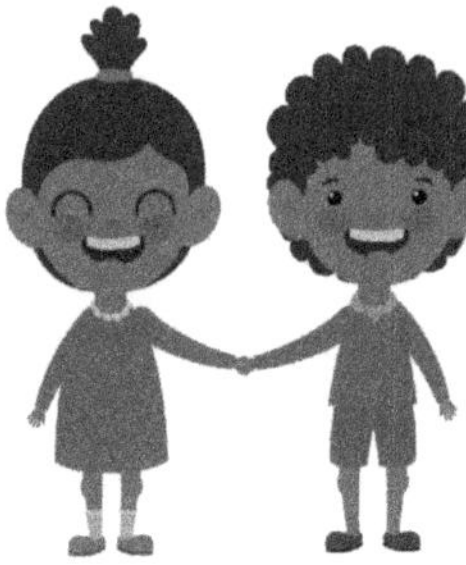

Travelling

Oh what places there may be
all of them I'd like to see
One has such a short life
Who knows if you get these chances in the
afterlife

The places I'd go
The things I'd see
A bit of time is all I need
A small chance
A little try
Please, somebody extend my life

I wish I could go to Paris
It almost makes me embarrassed
I haven't been places and by god's good graces
I just wish time could be in stasis

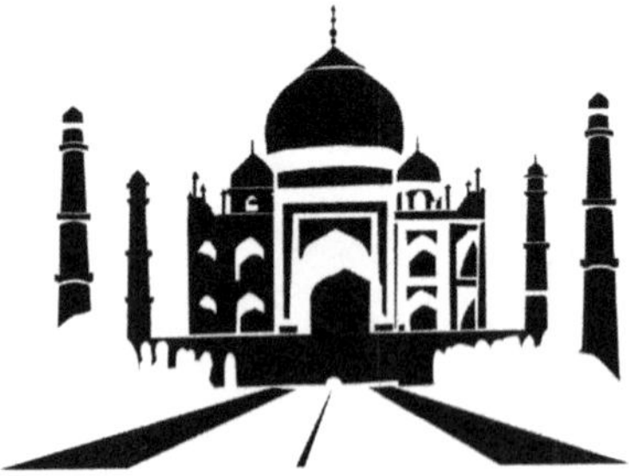

Culture

In this world there is so much
From plants to animals, from the Germans to the Dutch
It's time to stop and think about this
Reflect upon anything that you may miss

In the Americas you have pizza
move to Africa and you will find Tunisia
There are so many countries in this world
My brain is aching it feels like its been hurled

Soon we may have to stop
This is getting harder than I thought
We can move to Asia and japan
Then down to India, Madras then left to Pakistan

Now we could keep going for a long time
but good things come to an end
This sadly is the last poem
I hope you could share this with a friend

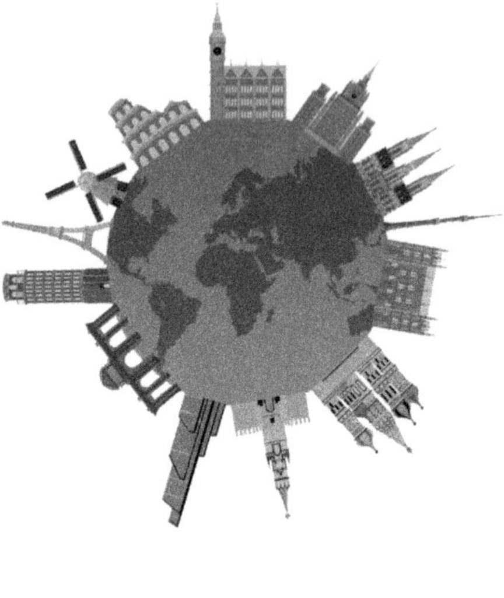

www.ingramcontent.com/pod-product-compliance
Lightning Source LLC
Chambersburg PA
CBHW051741130826
49812CB00033B/948
9789357211246